JIM   CLIFFORD

Increase Your Sales on eBay

Using NLP

(Neuro-Linguistic Programming)

CONTENTS

INTRODUCTION

INTRODUCTION

What is NLP?

NLP stands for Neuro-Linguistic Programming, a form of hypnosis based on **hidden, subliminally persuasive language patterns**, both spoken and written. NLP is used to indirectly or secretively persuade, sway, or control someone's subconscious mind and decision-making process without them ever being the wiser.

This Book was created for those who sell products on eBay who struggle to 'sell themselves,' and require ingenuity and creativity to write a great sales pitch. However, this guide will also be benefit those who do, in fact, 'sell themselves' well. If you are a seller, this guide is for you!

Using NLP, you create **a sales advantage over a competitor** selling the same product. There is nothing illegal about using NLP to sell your products. In fact, many major companies in today's world use these techniques all the time when selling products, or in other areas where persuasive language is important. Some of these companies have psychologists, psychiatrists, and even hypnotists in their marketing department.

Once you learn the techniques in this guide, you yourself will be more aware of these 'mind control' schemes and will be able to spot when someone else is using them. You will quickly take notice of commercials that are carefully scripted to sway viewers into thinking the way the advertiser wants them to think, and to act in a certain way as well. NLP techniques are not only effective on eBay. You can apply NLP to any area of life where **persuasive talk can make all the difference:** sales, social life, love life, school – just about anywhere communication occurs!

eBay is a huge marketplace. What better place than a worldwide, incredibly popular auction site to sell your goods and services! This being said, you must realize that you are not the only one trying to make a profit on eBay. You are competing not only with those who sell similar products, but also with every person that places an auction in the same section you do. It is a constant fight for customers' attention, and ultimately for their bid.

Using this NLP guide, you will gain an incredible advantage. Once you learn these techniques, they stay with you forever. **You will use NLP without even realizing it!** NLP will become natural to you. Tony Robbins, a master at motivational success and personal growth training, uses NLP as the HEART of his courses and seminars and of his entire system. You will become inspired simply by listening to him talk during his infomercials and seminars. Robbins helps people change their lives by showing them how to use NLP for personal growth, life management, depression, motivation, and much more – indeed, how to reprogram the mind to do what they want it to do.

Could you use this advantage on eBay?

We hope you enjoy using this information and benefiting from its applied use.

Thanks for reading!

ELICTING VALUES

Eliciting values will help you structure and tailor your NLP.

Here are some questions to ask when writing an ad copy:

- **What do they want?**
- **What do they like?**
- **What do they think they need?**
- **What do they think they deserve?**
- **What did they have in the past they want repeated?**
- **What did they have in the past they want avoided?**
- **What are they afraid of?**
- **What makes them happy?**

●What makes them sad?

When you write your ad description text dialogue, keep these questions in mind. Know your audience. Appeal to your target market. This cannot be stressed enough. Your bidders may have all sorts of issues that can make the difference in bidding on your auction or not.

Eliciting values is a technique that works most effectively in a live, 'person-to-person' situation. It's all about knowing your customers and making them happy through learning about their needs and wants. You want to satisfy your customers, right? Of course you do! They keep you in business.

To elicit values in person, shoot off a series of questions to your prospect. Each question should be carefully crafted to get answers that will enlighten your understanding of the customer before you. This will build a foundation to work from to tailor the rest of your NLP. Eliciting values on eBay, however, is trickier. You do not have direct contact with the customer, and so you must resort to other 'eliciting' tactics. The best way to get to know your potential customers on eBay is to research the categories you post your auctions in. Check out your competitors' auctions. What types of customer needs and wants do they address, if any? Also, look at buying patterns. These will tell you what people are going for, at what price, and more.

With a little analyzing, you can chart some market patterns. Use this information for the general format of your ad copy. Factor in bid price and reserve as well, based on your research. Addressing the needs and wants of your potential bidders is sure to spice up your next auction!

TRANCE WORDS

The words people put particular emphasis on or repeat frequently are their so-called trance words. By using the identical words they use, you will be able to tap directly into their consciousness and subconscious. After all, these are the words they think with and are most familiar with. After hearing you use them, people will feel you understand them completely.

An example of using trance words on eBay is to take what you estimate to be the most common words and phrases a person relates to, and then feed them back in a

17

slightly different way. When it comes to selling on eBay auctions, it is virtually impossible to know what a customer's personal trance words are without having ever spoken to them.

Therefore, we have compiled a list of a few 'common' trance words or 'power words' that provoke emotional states in people:

Absolutely.. Action.. Amazing.. Approved.. Attractive.. Authentic.. Bargain...Beautiful.. Better.. Big.. Bonus.. Colorful.. Colossal.. Complete.. Confidential.. Controversial.. Crammed.. Delivered.. Direct.. Discount..

Easily.. Endorsed.. Enormous..

Essential.. Excellent.. Exciting..

Exclusive.. Expert.. Explosive..

Extraordinary.. Extreme...

Famous.. Fascinating.. Fortune..

Free.. Full.. Genuine.. Gift..

Gigantic.. Greatest.. Guaranteed..

Helpful.. Highest.. Huge..

Immediately.. Immense..

Improved.. Incredible..

Informative.. Instructive.. Intense..

Interesting.. Largest.. Latest..

Lavishly.. Liberal.. Lifetime..

Limited.. Love.. Lowest.. Lucky..

Magic.. Mammoth.. Mega...

Miracle.. New.. Noted.. Odd..

Outstanding.. Personalized..

Popular.. Powerful.. Practical..

Professional.. Profitable..

Profusely.. Proven.. Quality..

Quickly.. Rare.. Reduced..

Refundable.. Remarkable..

Reliable.. Revealing..

Revolutionary.. Scarce.. Secrets..

Secure.. Security.. Selected..

Sense.. Sensational.. Simplified..

Sizable.. Special.. Startling..

Strange.. Strong.. Sturdy.. Suave..

Successful.. Superior.. Surprise..

Terrific.. Tested.. Tremendous..

Undeniably.. Unconditional..

Unique.. Unlimited..

Unparalleled.. Unsurpassed..

Unusual.. Useful.. Valuable..

Warm.. Wealth.. Weird..

Wonderful.

PRESUPPOSITIONS

Presuppositions are some of the most widely used "mind tricks" to steer someone into realizing what it is that they want, or what it is you want them to want... A "presupposition" is presented in tandem with a question, yet in order to answer the question, the customer must accept the accompanying presupposition. As such, presuppositions serve as a platform for **subliminal commands**.

Examples:

- "Would you like to (try our product) before (you buy it)?"
- "Would you like to (see what you are getting) before (you buy it)?"
- "Do you want to (get it now) or wait and (get it later)?"

Think of presuppositions as tactics that don't give a person a choice to decide 'yes' or 'no'. Rather, a presupposition indirectly chooses or decides upon a path for them.

Here are a few more examples of how a carefully crafted sentence can help sway a person towards the 'right' decision...or simply not leave them with much choice. Use these as a template to construct your own "decision-swayers."

Cause & Effect Presuppositions:

- "You won't get the most out of this product by reading about it since the best way to experience it is to experience it yourself."

Resistance-Breaking Presuppositions:

Using time distortions that bind comparable alternatives with the presupposition:

- "Won't it be great AFTER you get (your product) and you see for yourself (the buzz about your product)? Then you can look back, smile that smile of satisfaction, and think to yourself, that was one of the best bids I have ever placed!"

THOUGHT BINDING

- Setting up the thought direction; i.e., getting customers to recall what it's like to be in the mood you want them to be in.

- Giving subliminal commands to help customers stay in that mood while you have their attention.

- Manipulating decisions by using presuppositions during the thought-binding process.

Example of a non-thought-binding sales pitch:

"Lots of people like (this product) because it's fun, easy to use, and a great buy."

Example of a thought-binding sales pitch:

"Hey, did you ever see (this product), and just instantly know that you had to know more about (this product) and experience it for yourself? There was probably a time you were excited or intrigued about (something similar to your

27

product)... Imagine how great it will be to have (this product)..."

These subliminal statements create or recreate a certain mental state inside a person regarding the product at hand. Thought binding causes people to be more receptive to information about you and your product because you have set up and bound the direction of their thinking and their emotional processes. And the beauty is, they do not catch on to it because they find your sales pitch mesmerizing, emotionally appealing, and irresistibly interesting.

Remember: Every decision people make is dependent upon their state of mind. **If you want to change a customer's indecision, change their state of mind first**.

To effectively use some of the thought-binding techniques we've discussed, ask yourself the following questions:

• What different states of mind are people in when looking at your product? (Tired? Energetic? Happy? Sad?) See *Eliciting Values.*

• What is the final state you want them to be in?

- How can you make the state transition fun or enjoyable?

You can think of this process as building a chain of states, starting from the state they are currently in and building to the final state you want them to be in.

Let's say your customer is in a state of **indifference** about buying your product, which is often the case. And let's say the final state you want them in is **drooling with desire** to buy your product. Bit of a gap, huh? What you need to do is come up with an in-between state, such as **curiosity** or **intrigue**, using some of our thought-binding/presupposition techniques. You want them to look forward to buying or experiencing your product firsthand! So create mental states that facilitate that desire.

Bind their thoughts to YOU and YOUR PRODUCT.

BINDER COMMANDS

Binder commands are also known as subliminal messages/commands. They are an important part of your NLP technique.

Examples:

- "Right now, what you are getting in this fabulous (your product) is a time-limited offer..."

The subliminal message is "RIGHT NOW! GET THIS!"

- "This product is particularly suited for your needs, and if you buy it today you will receive our special 20% discount offer."

This incorporates a binder command of "DO IT! NOW! WITH THIS!"

It won't be long before you are able to whip up an archive of your own binder commands. Use these hand-in-hand with you application of thought binding and presuppositions. All of these together are how you construct your NLP language patterns.

TIME DISTORTION

Time distortion means having a person think about your product in conjunction with a time in the future, i.e. a future fantasy. Time distortion can also have binder commands imbedded within, thereby installing a subconscious 'need to fulfill' within an allotment of time. With effective thought binds, you can place anyone anywhere in time by directing their mind.

You can also use time distortion to induce security and trust in your product "six months from now."

People are always looking towards the future for countless things. Put your product in that picture!

PATTERNING

Basically, a pattern is where you use an entourage of NLP techniques in one script.

The value of patterns is the ability to lead someone to recall, imagine or experience wonderful feelings and states of mind through thought binding, while subconsciously linking them all to you and your product.

Patterns contain a set of devised words, references and timeframes seemingly having nothing to do with you and your product 'directly,' but subconsciously directed and linked very

36

specifically to both you and your product!

Use NLP patterns to capture your customers' attention, get them interested in your product (right now, or at the appropriate time), appeal to their various emotional and rational states, and issue subliminal commands to direct their thinking straight down the path you wish them to go... unwaveringly towards you, your product, and their wallet!

When writing a sales pattern, be sure to focus on your **trance words** and vivid adjectives as well. They help people think you connect with what they think, and you feel what they feel. They provoke the emotional and mental states you want your customers to experience; you then take advantage of these mind states by linking them to your product.

Many famous authors are masters of trance words. Take Stephen King, for example. In all of his books, he uses particular words to create the state of mind he wants his reader to be in.

So put yourself in the place of the customer: What do you, the customer, want to hear, want to feel, want to experience? What will sway this customer?

AUCTION TITLES

Using NLP in your auction titles is tricky due to the limited space you have. It can be done, but only to a small degree. If you are creative, you can use thought binding in a limited space, but this is easier said than done...

However, you can still set up mind states by choosing an auction title that deals with the state of mind you want people to have.

Many eBay sellers in the "Business for Sale" section use a rough version of thought binding. For instance, there are countless auctions for CDs and software items that will supposedly make you X amount of dollars reselling on eBay. These sellers select auction titles like, "Make eBay Your Career w/ this CD, 4K a Month; I did." This will attract more bids than, say, someone selling the same CD with an auction title like, "My CD Will Make You RICH."

Don't be bland! Set up a mind state in your title that people will picture in their mind.

One technique of good auction-title writing is playing on people's curiosity to the extreme. eBay is POWERED by curiosity, period. An auction title that makes no sense can be most effective, such as: "Bid Now or the Leprechaun Dies." People will wonder what the hell that is all about, and end up clicking to satisfy their curiosity.

Being overconfident in your auction title does well too, depending on how you implement it. For instance, stating: "You WILL Bid!" will make people want to see what you are demanding they "will" bid upon.

Remember, your auction title is the gateway to your auction. It is the door people will choose to go through or not, based on your auction title. Not only that, but you are competing with other sellers

41

who want buyers to look at their auction too. It helps to be creative and use your ingenuity as much as possible.

Be aware, the common practice on eBay is COPYCATTING. Once people notice an auction title (as well as items) of yours proving to be quite effective, they will follow right behind you and rip off your auction title. Don't worry; it happens all the time and there is little you can do about it. Sure, it is possible to 'copyright' an auction title, but it will prove to be more of a headache enforcing your copyright than you can imagine –

especially on eBay, the mother of online flea markets.

Using some of the common trance words coupled with thought-binding techniques can prove helpful in your auction titles, but due to the limited space, it is really quite hard to dish out full NLP in your auction title. It is best to write a title that will get the MOST attention, and then engage in your NLP skills in your description dialogue.

AD DESCRIPTION

Using NLP on eBay is very effective, but don't overdo it! Use common sense when applying NLP. Use it appropriately, in the right places, and you should do well.

Of course, NLP is not the only way to increase your auction successes. Obvious techniques like adding pictures, bonuses, free shipping, and emailing your old auction bidders about your new auctions are the common methods of improving your auction turnout.

When you write your NLP-laced ad description, formulate a plan, an **order of operations**.

Here is an example:

- **1st: Elicit Values** - Identify needs and wants.
- **2nd: Thought Binding -** Set up mental states, binding them to you and your product.
- **3rd: Presuppositions** - Influence the decision with 'trick' questions.
- **4th: Binder Commands: -** Use these throughout.

The above example is just that, an example. It is not written in stone as 'the' order of operations. You should think about your product, service, etc., coupled with your goals and how you want to appeal to your bidders, and go from there. Create your own order of operations. Keep in mind during all of these processes that you are executing patterns that include TRANCE WORDS and BINDER COMMANDS where possible.

ABOUT ME PAGE

What better place than your About Me page to let loose your new NLP skills?

If you do not already have an About Me Page on eBay, I suggest you create one. When eBayers notice another eBayer with an About Me page, quite a few of them will check it out. The About Me page is your permanent page on eBay where others can learn more about you and your auctions, give feedback, etc.

The best part about it is that it can be an effective marketing tool even when you have NO auctions listed! Perhaps you bid on an item on eBay, and other bidders are checking out the bid list. They may want to see who you are and what you're all about. Then you smack 'em with your slammin' NLP!

Increase Your Sales on eBay Using NLP

Recommended Readings

- Siddhartha by Hermann Hesse, www.bnpublishing.net

- The Anatomy of Success, Nicolas Darvas, www.bnpublishing.net

- The Dale Carnegie Course on Effective Speaking, Personality Development, and the Art of How to Win Friends & Influence People, Dale Carnegie, www.bnpublishing.net

- The Law of Success In Sixteen Lessons by Napoleon Hill (Complete, Unabridged), Napoleon Hill, www.bnpublishing.net

- It Works, R. H. Jarrett, www.bnpublishing.net

- The Art of Public Speaking (Audio CD), Dale Carnegie, wwww.bnpublishing.net

- The Success System That Never Fails (Audio CD), W. Clement Stone, www.bnpublishing.net